On Razor-Thin Tires

To Susan and Boyd
in friendship
Charles Halsted
June 2021

poems by

Charles Halsted

Finishing Line Press
Georgetown, Kentucky

On Razor-Thin Tires

For my older brother who kept me awake
as I drove through the night
Thomas A. Halsted
1933-2017

ACKNOWLEDGMENTS

The author gratefully acknowledges the publications in which these poems
and an essay first appeared:

Blood and Bourbon: "On Razor-Thin Tires"
The Ekphrastic Review: "The Boozy Soldier" (published as "The Merry
        Drinker")
Evening Street Press: "Boxed In," "The Dawn Freight"
Hektoin International: "The Korean Soldier" (essay)
Medusa's Kitchen: "Myosotis"
Montana Mouthful: "Forest Dragon" (published as "Dragon in the Forest")
The Moon Magazine: "Same Species"
Poetry Now: "Hummingbird"
Rosette Maleficarum: "My Garden of Delights"

Publisher: Leah Huete de Maines
Editor: Christen Kincaid
Cover Art: Bob Waldman, 1936 Dodge photo, "Cascadia Classic"
Author Photo: Cindy Davis; http://www.cindydavisphotography.com/
Cover Design: Cindy Davis; http://www.cindydavisphotography.com/

Order online: www.finishinglinepress.com
        also available on amazon.com

Author inquiries and mail orders:
Finishing Line Press
P. O. Box 1626
Georgetown, Kentucky 40324
U. S. A.

Table of Contents

STORMY WEATHER

BECOMING AND BEING A PHYSICIAN

EKPHRASIS

COMING OF AGE

Forest Dragon

Near the end of summer of 1942, just four feet tall
two months before turning six years old, my
father took our family to vacation at Honnedaga Lake,

an Adirondack gem twenty miles from the
nearest town, my Pa driving the family car
along an ancient curvy and potholed dirt road.

We stayed in my paternal grandfather's old
house on the shore where Pa had spent his
childhood summers, a starting point for a hike

to a well-hidden lake at the end of a winding
trail through a dark forest that teemed with
strange scary animals, or so we were told.

Midway through our month-long stay, my
parents, older brother, two sisters, and I
set out on the three-mile hike to the well-

hidden lake, where my father would teach my
siblings and me how to catch one or more deep-
swimming trout, then to bring them to an

ancient cabin on the shore where he would show
us how to scoop out their guts, to ready their
flesh to for frying and eating.

A mile or so along the trail, my mother at my side, I
heard a gentle rustling and mewling sound, then found
a foot-long brown-and-white speckled baby fawn.

As I bent over to stroke its head and sides, we heard a
nearby growling noise. A fuming dragon, maternal instincts
aroused, crashed through the trees in full protective mode.

Without a second thought, my mother picked a five-foot stick from the ground, nearly as thick as a baseball bat, and swung it into the shoulder of the charging doe.

With hearts racing, we stood aside as the just-tamed mother deer nuzzled her baby fawn back into the thicket, my childhood saved by my Mum.

Overseas

We stand on the lawn in the fall of '42,
trees bare, river and murky marshland beyond.
My family poses together before our Pa goes
off to a faraway place called Overseas.

Her hand on my six-year-old shoulder, Mum
gazes past big sister's hair at the love of
her life in full uniform, knowing that soon
he'll be gone from us all.

Resplendent in his US Army coat, an
officer's hat with spread-winged eagle over
the bill, a new dark tie and a resolute smile, my
Pa is ready to leave, to care for wounded soldiers.

He carries my four-year-old sister who's
bundled up against the cold, her head
resting on his shoulder. Holding back her
tears, she fears he will never come home.

My two older siblings stand proudly by, one on
each side of Mum, big sister almost eleven,
sure she can handle it all, big brother age nine,
soon to be the boy in charge.

I stand in front of the rest, anxious, solemn,
no trace of a smile. Soon Pa will be gone,
none of us knows for how long. Though Mum
will care for us all, I am already alone.

How Superman Kept Me Safe

When I was a child in World War II,
my Pa was a soldier overseas.
I never knew if he'd come home,
whether the Krauts would invade

from the nearest beach ten miles away,
whether I'd ever grow up. Whooping
sirens would tell us when it was time to
leave, but I never knew where we would go.

The scratchy news of the day came from the
family Victrola-radio to which I anxiously tuned
each afternoon when I returned from school.
The newspaper store downtown always carried

the latest comic books that assured me
that I was safe, since either Superman or
Batman could vanquish all invaders,
especially any bayonet-toting Krauts.

Forty years later, with a family of my own,
my teenage son informed me that if my mother
had not made me toss out my Superman comics,
they might now be worth a million bucks.

Little did he know their real value: that
Superman kept me safe from invading Krauts.

Mister Chips Was My Muse

My favorite childhood pet
helped make me who I am.
I named him Mister Chips.

Though he was the family cat,
he took to me the most, jumped up
on my bed when it was time to sleep,

crawled under my covers to warm me,
to inform me that I was his favorite
human being in the whole world.

He must have read the news; he knew all
that was going on. His presence made me
confident, always made me tops in school.

Though he's been gone for more than
seventy years, I still remember him as
my know-it-all muse.

The Closet at the Top of the Stairs

Born the third of four children, never the heir,
from infancy through his earliest years
he was taught he should never go near
the closet in the attic at the top of the stairs
where a dark hairy monster dwelt in its lair.
Known as the Googeebocky, a creature of fear,
it could gobble up the smallest ones,
the children most easy to scare.

Full grown with children of his own,
he learned that a demon cancer had appeared
that would consume his body if not cut clear.
He feared anesthesia, since once in the dark
he'd be face to face with the monster, still
ready to devour him in a single swill.

Beware the Jabberwock!

The claws that snatch! This is old stuff.
My mother knew every word cold, could recite
it at the drop of a hat. Just say Wock! and

she'd be off and running, ensuring that
each of her children knew that the Jabberwock,
the monster who dwelled at the darkest end of

the closet at the top of the attic stairs, should be
the one most feared. But its equally scary
companion was the frumious Bandersnatch

who guarded the closet door. You were doomed
if you turned the key in the lock. With one
more step you would never grow up, except,

if and only if, you promised you would
forever be good, for only then could you
be saved by the slithy toves, gyring and

gimbling in the wabe, at the ready
to vanquish the Jabbersnatch, bury
its corpse by the Tum Tum tree.

Hitler's Mustache

The game was over one week before the
Nazis surrendered the seventh of May '45.
Hitler huddled in a bunker with his former
mistress Eva Braun, now his wife of one day.

They made a suicide pact: She would go first.
After she popped a huge dose of cyanide, Hitler
unholstered his Luger, placed the barrel tip
against his soft palate, squeezed the trigger.

The blast caused the hair on his head to fly
from its roots. Only der Fuhrer's mustache
remained. If you go to Berlin, you can visit

the field where invading Soviets burned their
remains. No one will tell you exactly where,
lest modern-day Nazis make it a shrine.

My Viking Ancestry

Halsted means several things:
Hal for Prince Hal, future English
king, who went from Falstaff protégé

to Henry V who conquered France.
There's also a Halstead, England.
(Oh, why did they misspell my name?)

It you travel to the Sognefjord in Norway,
there's Hyllestad not far from its mouth,
whereas there's a Hallestad in Sweden and even a

Halsted in Denmark. These seem to clinch
it, since the Vikings conquered southern
England and much of Ireland centuries ago.

Once on a train in southern England, the
woman across the aisle asked me
"Viking or Norman?" both conquering

peoples of Britain a thousand years or so ago.
She told me I was descended from Vikings,
as proven by my high cheekbones.

That sounded good enough, but only explained
my father's name. Family lore says my mother's
forebears came to England in the Norman invasion.

Great-Grandfather Mined for Gold*

A found poem from inherited letters

September 1855, Potters Bar, California

Dear Mama,

The land is mountainous and filled with brooks
that dash away with cold clear water. Sitting
under a big oak on a velvet cushion of moss,
I can gaze at a stream of rolling pebbles, look
out on the green distant valley of the Sacramento.

The Digger tribe are poor wretches who live
on worms and roots. Though they look like devils,
they are harmless, dressed only in dirty blankets.
Their faces are painted with crossbars, and
sticks are stuck in their long shaggy hair.

They smoke out grasshoppers that jump into
a circle of pits, or else are roasted on top,
to be saved for winter desserts after repasts
of lizards and slimy snails.

On Sunday afternoons it is the custom for
some of my friends needing exercise to
go out and kill the miserable natives who
live in the nearby forests.

I shall send up to Oregon to get a little
Injun boy. I do not like negro slavery,
but a Flathead is different.

---

* According to Benjamin Madley (*An American Genocide*), about eighty
percent of native Californians were killed by white settlers between 1846
and 1873.

Baseball Achilles

When I looked down from the left-field stands at
Fenway Park, age nine in '46, I could watch my
hero Ted Williams patrol the Boston Red Sox
outfield when the other team was at bat.

Ted could field as well as he hit: his batting
averaged .406 in '41, still the all-time best. Back
from World War II in '46, he hit a 502-foot homer,

the longest-ever at Fenway Park. It bounced off the
head of a middle-aged fan, a construction engineer,
whose outfield seat became a permanent shrine.

Yet, in his only World Series in '46, Ted injured
his elbow and missed two games. He batted a
dismal .200, far below his season average, and
the Red Sox succumbed to the St. Louis Cardinals.

My Father's Flyrod

hangs off three hooks screwed high in the wall
behind the chair in my study, so all I need to do
is glance at it from time to time to recall when
he taught me how to fish when I was ten years old.

With three-foot bamboo sections times three,
the way flyrods were made in those days from
mysteriously split Asian trees, it was a magic
wand to conjure up a fish from the deep by

catapulting a sinking fake fly at the tip of a
line into a fathomless lake, near tree-covered
shade where a bug-mistaken trout would
patiently lurk, ready to pounce on its prey.

The line was coiled in a round steel reel at
the hand-held butt end, waiting to unwind
with every cast of the line, to the end of which
had been tied a fake fly.

Each of three rod sections with interlocking ends
played a singular role: the butt to be held, midsection
to extend, and flexible tip to assure a perfect cast of
the line through seven tiny even-spaced rings.

My father taught me how to cast in an Adirondack lake, but
my catching success came forty years later, when I
replaced his bamboo flyrod, a relic, with a fiberglass
wand to lure trout from the currents of western streams.

The Letter

"It's only a letter," my Pa said to me, just
thirteen. He'd been gone in the War and lost
to us all till he returned in '45. Five years later
he upended our family with a move to LA.

"It's best we separate," said his letter to my
Mum. "But why?" I said with welling tears.
I chose to remain and grow up in LA, while
Mum, shattered, returned to her eastern roots.

For the next two years, I had Pa to myself, spellbound
by his research tales. As an adult, I followed him in
a medical career, married twice. I divorced my
first wife when our children were all in their teens.

Crashing Waves

When I go to bed at the North Shore estate,
ours since great-grandfather returned from
the Civil War, I hear distant waves breaking
and crashing on the granite shore,

sloshing up sloping rock to a tidepool and washing
out the tiny creatures dwelling there, then receding
through the rocks, grinding across the bottom
pebbles and rolling them out to sea.

When the moon is full and the tide is high,
the incoming sea crashes to crescendo after
about sixty waves. By then I've stopped counting,
I'm lulled into sleep.

Shades of Green

After studying painting in his twenties in 1890s
Paris, my maternal grandfather Packa portrayed
World War I victors—a Japanese statesman and
the premiers of Serbia and Romania.

Later sitters were Harvard professors, President
Coolidge, Chief Justices Hughes and Holmes,
Eastman of Kodak, E. E. Cummings as baby and child,
his own family, including me, his namesake grandson.

His style was to create, not imitate,
to think and paint simultaneously what
he saw and how he felt, to show what
he called "true reverence" for beauty.

At age nine, I stood on a stool to gaze from
his attic studio at the landscape I'd seen in his
watercolor paintings: bushes, rocks, and trees
stretching down to the breaking waves of the sea.

When Packa asked what colors I saw, I jumped
to the vastness of green life before the sea. He
replied: "Which colors of green? How many
greens does nature provide those bushes and trees?"

Then he brought out his color wheel, a spinning
surface for blending paints, to show the greens
in nature just as they were, with different mixtures
of yellow and blue, creating just the right hue

for each bush or tree. He showed me the colors
of the rolling sea, from deep to light green before
the crash of each wave into foam on the shore.

When I turned twenty-one, Packa gave me
me five hundred dollars, so I could discover
the Paris that once he knew.

Sailing with Packa

Strolling through Amsterdam's Van Gogh Museum, I came
upon "Seascape at Les Saint Maries-de-la-Mer," painted
by the master two years before he died in 1890,
depicting sailboats off the French Mediterranean shore.

Three boats move innocently upon a dark blue sea
well beyond the foreground of rolling waves, their urgent
white foam roiling the surface, their breaking points
marked by slanting streaks of dark blue.

Gazing at the Van Gogh seascape, I recalled that Packa, my
maternal grandfather, had studied art in Paris in the 1890s.
Although a portrait painter, Packa's forte was watercolors of New
England's northeastern shore where he lived most of his years.

Back home, I studied Packa's watercolors that I inherited.
Sure enough, his painting that hangs near my desk depicts
a rough seascape with two gaff-rigged sailboats and two
lobstermen in a rowboat preparing to lower their traps.

In the foreground, rolling green waves become roiling white foam,
their breaking points marked by diagonal streaks of dark blue.

Portrait of Me as a Wrangler

My maternal grandfather, after whom I am named,
painted poets, professors, presidents, and each of his
children and grandchildren, including me when I was fifteen.

I'd just finished ten weeks working on a dude ranch in the
Sierra Nevada mountains of California, two hundred miles
from where I grew up in LA, a place completely different
from the New England coast where my grandfather lived.

The portrait shows me with a feathered hat, not really
a cowboy but cocky all the same, with solemn face,
clasped bony-knuckled hands, and Levi jacket partly open.

I must have been thinking about the pack trip I'd led to
a mountain meadow in a train of eight horses, each
carrying a city dude who depended on me to be sure
the horses behaved, that no one was thrown off a cliff.

I know I was thinking about the woman twice my age
who assumed I was older and ripe for her picking.
Since then, I have wondered what might have transpired
if I had said yes to her proposal.

My Seventeenth Year

I turned seventeen in October 1953
when *From Here to Eternity* was the
number-one hit, and Ike commanded
an arsenal of nuclear weapons, just in case.

We had launched the first nuclear sub when
Marilyn Monroe married Joe DiMaggio, about
the same time as my high school girlfriend agreed
to go steady and we progressed to deep kissing.

We agreed to keep it all above the waist,
the expected teenage norm in those days,
while the US raced with the Soviets to
develop the first successful hydrogen bomb.

February saw the first polio vaccine and
Nasser proclaimed his premiership of Egypt.
March saw the French defeat in Vietnam, while
my steady and I agreed we'd never "go all the way."

In mid-April, my college acceptance letter
arrived. Bill Haley recorded "Rock Around
the Clock," while *The Seven Samurai* and Brando's
On the Waterfront were top movie hits.

Roger Bannister, a tireless Brit, ran the first four-
minute mile on May 6 and I determined to become
a future college jock, practiced long-distance running
through the treeless hills that surround UCLA.

Frustrated with my steady, I parked on Mulholland Drive
with a "bad girl," looking down on the lights of LA. My
attempts to "go all the way" were rebuffed. The Supreme
Court banned public school segregation the very next day.

That summer before college, Elvis came out with
"That's All Right," his first hit, while I was a busboy
in a fancy hotel in Santa Monica. Though I had joined a
union, the waitresses only passed on ten cent tips.

On Razor-Thin Tires

On a cross-country trip at sixteen, I gazed up at Lincoln in DC
by moonlight, while my brother, nineteen, and two more
guys waited, engine running, in our '36 Dodge, all
tires worn razor thin, taking two-hour shifts
at the wheel, though my big brother
stayed awake on my turns just in
case I screwed up while we
careened through the night, arriving
next day for an overnight stay in New Orleans,
Mecca at the Mississippi's mouth, where at evening
we strolled along Bourbon, the street paved with sin, partying
tourists tossing trinkets from ancient wrought-
iron balconies, until we reached a half-
open door, where a sleazy guy with
a deep Southern drawl urged
us into a kind of place I'd never been
before, where my big brother showed me
how to belly up to the bar, order one beer while ten
older men, no wives, watched a strip-dancer take off all her
clothes, and the trick was to make your beer last just
as long as her dance.

Cardinal Sweater

When I ran the freshman two-mile race, I lettered,
third place. Now one of the jocks, a Cardinal sweater
was my reward. Next year I was lapped, followed coach's
instructions, veered off the track, decided to quit.

Fifty years later, alma mater appeals appear,
always opening with "Dear Student Athlete."
I made sure my sons knew of my freshman success,
that they be proud of their Dad was my secret wish.

Last year my grandson, a high-school athlete, asked
me for my best two-mile time, still lodged in my memory.
"Awesome time, Grandad," was my glorious reward.

Every now and then, I sneak a peek at my red sweater.
It's still in my drawer, the year's number now lost,
but nevertheless a reminder of my past athletic success.

Myosotis

Ne m'oubliez pas, do not forget me, she spoke
in soft voice of the mountain flowers of France,
myosotis—forget-me-nots. Together we wove a
garland of flowers for her hair.

Young volunteers, we worked in a tiny alpine
village. A larger-than-life wooden crucifix
hung under the roof of the church.

We climbed the nearby mountain with villagers on
their saint's day to a chapel near a lake in the sky,
held hands all the way down, that summer of '58.

For two weeks we spoke her language without end,
French writers and philosophers from Voltaire to Camus—
the meanings of our lives now and to come. Our minds
and souls commingled with the mountain flowers.

On sputtering motorbike, I was off to my future,
my other world. My first real love stayed behind.
I never turned back.

Do you still go to that little village so far away?
Je ne t'ai jamais oublié, I never forgot you,
ma myosotis.

GROWN UP

The News from Venus

Tonight's news
from Venus
is neither sad
nor glad the mind
responds to images
though the world
unravels in choppy
phrases the newest
songs become
ingrained in minds
like ancient tomes
stored in the attic
their omnipresent odor
of rotten eggs
the entire effect
a harsh awakening
to meaningless
reality directed neither
inward towards
ourselves nor outward
to spaces between
the stars reeling
endlessly beyond
comprehension
to vast unknown
reaches of the universe

JFK Remembered

One of my colleagues told me the news:
He had been cut down in Dallas,
the hellhole near the center of America.

I recalled the day three years before
when I had stood in a jam-packed room
in a downtown hotel in Rochester, New York,

the city where I was attending medical school.
Suddenly a cry from the crowd: "He's here!"
A phalanx of bodyguards pushed us to one side.

Three feet away, beads of sweat on his brow,
slight smile, hands outstretched, he touched the
nearest of us as he walked past. He gave a short

uplifting speech, the crowd dispersed, and he was
gone. On inauguration day nine weeks later, he
told me to ask myself what I could do for my country.

The Day He Died

"He's been shot!" my lab mate said, at 12:30 PM, CST,
11/22/63. I stood at the counter pipetting a solution,
the first experiment of my new career.

We all stopped what we were doing, descended the stairs
to the residents' lounge, watched the horror unfold on
a fuzzy black-and-white TV.

Someone had filmed the assassination and its aftermath:
how Oswald had found his way to the sixth floor
of the Texas School Book Depository in Dallas,

how a single shot blew off the top of my President's
head, the first one I had ever voted for. We all
thought the assassination was a plot by LBJ,

who was quickly sworn in, Jackie a witness in her blood-
stained pink suit. Less than two years later, we invaded
Vietnam. From then on, nothing seemed the same.

Boom Box

In the heyday of the Beatles, a few months before the '67
Arab-Israeli War, I bought a boom box in the Athens PX
and brought it back to Cairo, where I was stationed at
the US Naval Medical Research Unit Number 3.

By then we had seen most of the nearby sights—the Sphinx,
the Great Pyramids, and the graves of the famous pharaohs.
We decided to venture further south of Cairo to Saqqara
to explore the tombs of the bulls at the Serapeum.

From 1300 BC to 30 AD, ancient Egyptians worshiped
sacred bulls in Luxor, floated their dead bodies 400 miles
down the Nile to Saqqara, and laid each lifeless bovine to rest
in its own room in a quarter-mile circular mausoleum.

During our visit, a single string of ceiling lights welcomed
foreign tourists, who in turn provided baksheesh for the
descendants of ancient Egyptians.

I carried my boom box armed with the latest
Beatles' hits, wondering if the ghosts of the
sacred bulls were enjoying "A Hard Day's Night."

Saturday Morning at the Cairo Bazaar

Arabic voices resounded off walls, throngs of
tourists milled along winding narrow alleyways,
donkey-drawn peasants' carts careened, and
shopkeepers stood in doorways, proclaiming
their ancient wares to passing American tourists.

I frequently visited Mohammed's shop, where I
procured an antique chest bound around all sides
with golden trim, a wooden plate inlaid with a
pattern of ivory stars, and two small wooden end-
tables, each with an intricate pattern under glass.

One Saturday morning when I arrived at his shop,
Mohammed proposed half-off on any one item
I sought, my part to pretend an expensive bargain,
bid up against any gullible American who would
soon pay full price for the most expensive item.

Sure enough, an unsuspecting tourist strolled in, cast
his eyes on an ancient harem screen complete with
hinged peekaboo openings for balconied wives to view
their common husband below with his friends. The tourist
proclaimed it a steal at one thousand Egyptian pounds.

During this transaction, I had grown enamored of
the ancient wooden screen, secretly hoped the tourist
would give up and leave. Once the tourist had gone,
Mohammed went to the back, brought out another,
let me have it at half price.

Lost Luggage

Rushing to make the next plane out from
Cairo, I was directed to toss my
suitcase onto a pile of look-alikes.

In my haste, I forgot the cardinal rule
of Egyptian life: always tip those in need
who exist on a much lower rung than me.

My destination was Copenhagen, where
I was due to meet my wife for a jaunt
through several European cities.

Once landed and off to baggage claim,
I waited at the conveyer belt in vain.
Each bag looked about the same.

None resembled my brown leather bag,
a sturdy companion of more than ten years,
the only suitcase I had brought.

The airline people said they would do their
best to help, cabled urgent messages over
land and sea to the airport in Cairo.

All to no avail. Six weeks went by. Back
home in the States, I got a call from the airport
in Sacramento. My missing bag had been found.

It had never been opened. Even though I had
neglected his baksheesh, the impoverished
bag handler in Cairo would never steal.

The Mystic in Our Midst

He sits on a bench in front of the market,
stares transfixed at what I cannot know,
wearing sandals and thick white cotton pajamas,

perhaps to reflect the heat of summer or to
keep him warm in winter's cold. He appeared
in our town six months ago, now roams street

after street from one end to the other. Under
one arm, he carries a Bible, a Koran, or perhaps a
tome read by Buddhists or other Eastern mystics.

Is he here to bless or curse, to convert or disdain?
He seems quite harmless, just somewhat strange.

From my window I see our town mystic,
clothed all in white, marching with fixed
intention along the street near my home.

When he reaches my house, he turns, walks
up the path through my flowers and trees. I
I must quickly decide what I must do next.

The Guy Next Door

When we moved in four years ago, wives brought casseroles,
their husbands shouted greetings. Solid wooden fences
between houses should make for good neighbors.

My new study overlooks the front yard, where a red-berried
hedge blocks out the driveway next door—except at its end
where protrudes the hood of an ancient rusted-out pickup truck.

My next-door neighbor strides up the street as soon as
the mail truck comes into view. He wears a foreign
legion hat with flaps covering his ears and neck.

Braving Sahara sandstorms, he marches toward
the mailbox, taking care to avoid all neighborly
contact. When I walk out, he crosses the street,

avoids any chance to converse. When I simply offer
"Good morning," he grunts and marches on. We take
turns removing our mail, neither making a sound.

Last October near Halloween, a fake human skeleton
appeared with a full toothy grin in the driver's seat of
the rusted-out truck, its bony hands grasping the wheel.

With firm voice, I asked him to take it away, lest it frighten
my visiting granddaughter out of her wits. Speaking to me
for the first time, he said, "Sure." It was gone the next day.

A few months later, hearing high-pitched backyard chatter, I
peeked through a crack in our fence and saw a swing and a slide
for small children. I learned from my neighbor across the street

that the guy and his wife ran a weekly playground for kids.
Soon after, I chatted briefly with his pleasant wife as she
trimmed their front-yard flowers.

Last week, returning my greeting, he told me about
the new solar roof panels he had just had put in. The ice
has been broken, though we have yet to utter our names.

Sweet Caroline

If you go to Fenway Park to watch
my beloved Boston Red Sox, you'll
hear it after they've passed the
seventh inning stretch, or

sometimes even before when the Sox
are only a run or two behind. From
somewhere behind the Green Monster,
that sheer green wall behind left field,

a divine voice will envelop the stands—
Neil Diamond singing the song that's
known by all Sox fans, "Sweet Caroline."

Written to a throbbing beat, the song
that played at Fenway for more than two
decades is so well known that all
Red Sox fans sing right along.

If the Sox are behind, "Sweet Caroline"
almost always works. They are bound to
bounce right back, either tie or win the
game when they take to the field again.

Downsizing

Our yard's too big, too much grass to be mown,
two stories for two climbing upstairs and down.
All it takes is one slip and decline from then on.
We'd better downsize before we're too old.

Yet, the sun sets on the far western hills.
From floor to ceiling a lifetime of books
defines my present with more to fulfill.
Tomorrow's dawn will turn darkness to gold.

My Garden of Delights

My garden is one of earthly delights.
Its just-turned loam, warmed by sun,
fertilizes creatures that dwell within.

Between flowering trees of dormant fruit,
spiders weave intricate webs, traps
for voyeurs who may happen by.

Preening lilacs and redbuds weave in the breeze,
while thick-stemmed succulents stand upright,
blooming for passersby who stop to admire.

The pale purple primrose and orange poppies
lean gently towards the brightening sun,
await pollination by patrolling bees.

The furry flesh of the golden yarrow
resting gently by the garden wall
invites gentle strokes.

The kumquat tree is heavy with fruit,
ready to pluck for the suck of its juice,
while the opened trumpets of bright red salvia

entice penetration by hummingbird beaks.
Each bird hovers close for its turn.

Backyard Jungle

My backyard is a jumble of species of
birds, some migratory, others native, dodging
squirrels darting to and fro. I have placed
two feeders fifty feet apart, with birdseed to

attract finches, juncos, warblers, and sparrows
that sail in to compete for food. With my nozzled
garden hose, I blast clean my stone birdbath,
then fill it to the top.

This afternoon, my yard falls silent, birds in
flight, squirrels gone. A yellow-streaked cat
plods slowly through. Suddenly, my neighbor's
chainsaw growls.

Dusk Detail

Chirping sparrows congregate, barely seen
under red-berried toyon bushes. Squawking
crows crowd treetops on our late Sunday

walk along our town's empty perimeter ditch,
lined by ancient eucalypti, bare cottonwoods
reaching toward the sky.

A ditch-spanning bridge ends at a farmer's pond
where honking geese sojourn in winter,
and green-helmeted mallards trail in pairs.

A great egret stands still at the shore till it
sights a fish, plunges its head below the
water's surface. About once a week, a hard

winter rain fills the narrow side ditch that runs
west to east before entering the southwest-flowing
river before it empties into the ocean bay.

At eye level across the ditch, the
receding sun lingers over the tops
of the coast range hills.

Finch Feeder

Suspended from a branch of an oak just fifteen
feet from my window hangs a wire mesh
feeder filled with finch food.

Seven inches high, two inches wide, it encases a
coveted pillar of seeds within its tiny mesh sides,
held in place by metal plates that cover each end.

I doubted the finches would show after the torrential
rain through the night. To my surprise, five fluttered
in, settled on a branch six feet above ground, now

bare in winter cold. There's space for four birds at once,
each plucking seeds through miniscule holes.
Though finches all and more than one kind, they

jostle each other, sometimes upside down. Most
common is the goldfinch, then the purple or rosy,
all four to six inches long with triangular beaks.

Each bird tries to peck out the most, to ward off all
the others. The excluded birds hover anxiously by,
ready to claim the next vacated spot.

If I walk out through our front door, they scatter
to the treetops, then flutter back to their rightful
places once I am safely inside.

Hummingbird

Eating breakfast soon after dawn, I hear
a whirring sound, a tiny bird midair:

magenta helmet, shiny green back,
vibrating wings, not three feet away,
seeking nectar from salvia in bloom.

What miracle sent you, suspended midair, to
enchant me on this day? Is it all in your DNA?

Buzzing Bee

A noisy pool party roars behind a leafy hedge as
I walk our town's perimeter pathway to identify
birds, plants, insects, ducks and other waterfowl.

Near the trail, a humming bee flits among
the purple petals of a mountain mock vervain.
I lean in to inhale its fragrance. The bee buzzes a
warning an inch from my ear, returns to its task.

Continuing along the winding pathway, I cross
a wooden bridge to reach two farmers' ponds
about one hundred yards apart.

Through my binoculars I spy two Canada geese
teaching five trailing goslings to swim. A green-
headed mallard cruises near shore, guards the
brown-feathered spouse at his side.

Not far from shore, two hard-shelled turtles sun
themselves on a log, occasionally dipping their heads
below water's surface to sample drifting morsels of food.

At the second pond, a snow-white great egret straightens
its angular neck, raises its powerful wings, and flaps
along the shore seeking foolish near-surface fish.

I turn to walk slowly home, careful to avoid
touching the oak-like leaves in clusters
of three beside the asphalt path.

I, Volcanic Rock,

lay dormant two
thousand feet below
the surface of the earth
awaiting eruption
for upwards of an eon
or a billion years
that's a thousand million
just a quarter of the time
since the sun cast
out the earth to fend
for itself in the
vast universe and
as the earth whirled
around the sun
cracks appeared about
a mile deep
forming magma
from shifting massive
plates that
shot me to the
surface to erupt
as a hot plume that cooled
to become a solid black rock
with smooth shiny sides,
four inches long
two inches wide
weighing a pound
and one half on
your bathroom scales
you found me in
one zillionth
of a geologic instant
picked me off the ground
asked your friend
the geology prof
where I was from
the nearest volcano

about one hundred
miles away which is
zero in geological
space or time and
here I survive as a
paperweight on your
desk surviving you both

The Coming Apocalypse

Strolling downtown, I passed a building
entrance alcove that two homeless men had
transformed into an encampment, their sleeping
bags and backpacks piled against the door.

I had met Richard before, when I volunteered
to assist in our town's winter shelter. His wife
had kicked him out, but his daughter would
graduate this year from medical school in Mexico.

Now did not seem a good time for the handout
Richard's companion eagerly sought. I shook each
one's hand, wished them well, continued on my way.

At the crosswalk, I watched our town mystic,
clad only in a white cloak, rapidly crossing
the street, an apparition with an unknown goal.

Tomato Truck Revenge

As if in flight, a madman in a Porsche tore
across two lanes to cut me off. I should have
given him the finger, but by then he was far

out of sight. After my wife calmed me down,
I recalled my classmate's story from the Traffic
Offender's School I'd attended twenty years before.

This guy—who claimed to be an expert driver—
was driving a long tomato truck on Interstate 5
when a jerk in an open Chevy convertible sped up
and cut him off just to prove some manhood point.

The tomato truck guy waited until the next
rightward curve, pulled his load to the center
lane, veered sharply left, dumped dozens of
of ripe tomatoes into the Chevy's open cab.

My story was quite tame: I was pulled over
in town for going forty in a twenty-five-mile
zone. They let me off easy with a $50 fine
and an entertaining afternoon at Traffic School.

Old School Appeal

Lying innocent in my mailbox, the New
England prep school address, top left, gave its
purpose away. But how could they remember
me when I had left them at age thirteen?

I could have thrown the envelope away unopened,
but a smidgen of childhood remembrance drove
my curiosity. I was hooked. I ripped off the
left-side margin, slid out the perfectly folded

appeal, the enduring school emblem embossed
top left. Scanning the page, I read Class of '54,
completely ignoring the fact that my family had
moved cross-country to Los Angeles in 1950.

How nice, they wish me a happy birthday. They
even have the day and year of my birth.
Then I recalled that I had played left tackle on
our eighth-grade Midgets football team,

especially the game where I was mowed
over by the much taller kid on the
opposing team, allowing their five-foot
quarterback to push on through to score.

They beat us by one or two touchdowns,
I could not remember which. Nevertheless,
I found the return envelope, wrote my old
prep school their requested check.

Current Swirls

in circles, fosters bubble lines that continue
endless journeys over eons of time and
shifting rocks, sustaining insect lives.

Barely downstream of the last current swirl
lurks one or more primordial trout from eons
of spawn, ever seeking floating insects
to sustain generations of its species.

At the opposite end of the survival chain,
standing on land near the current swirl, I
slowly raise my fiberglass wand to which I've
reeled a barely seen line, where at its end

I have tied a fake floating hooked fly, the
better to deceive a lurking creature into
the edge of the onrushing stream, to
grab my hook and seal its doom.

To do so, I must make a perfect cast of
my line so that the fake fly lands in
the stream at the edge of the swirl.

I repeat with intention every new cast,
seeking space just inches downstream from the
last, for only my skill will induce the primordial
creature to dart from the deep, make its grab.

Holding tight to my line, I slowly reel
in my prize, lay its head on a rock, bash
its small brain, take knife to its belly,
scoop out its guts, take it home to my bride.

O, Oncorhynchus

You swim sexless for years in deep Pacific
darkness to Japan and back, dodging fishnets,
trawlers, whales, seeking the mouths
of the rivers of your birth.

At high tide you jump sand barriers, swim
upstream at least fifty miles, leap waterfalls,
change colors and shapes to reach the calm
waters where you were first hatched.

Your splashing tails carve pits in shallow gravel
to hide your eggs, bright red, by the dozens. Your
male suitors charge with snapping jaws, to become
the first one to cover your eggs with milky sperm.

Then you die. Your putrid rotting carcasses line the
shallows at the shore, your larvae occupy the rocky
river bottoms. Your surviving fingerlings emerge
full grown and cross the endless freezing ocean.

During years of seagoing, saltwater flows through their
anadromous veins until they return to the fresh waters of
their birth, unless they have been eaten by seals, bears,
or humans transforming their flesh to their own.

Same Species

His supplicant hands clasped as in prayer,
head fully hooded, face barely seen,
a thin pinkish blanket over his back,
he's barely protected from winter cold,

invisible to the disdaining suits ten feet away who
march with fixed purpose, carefully avoid even
a sideways glance toward this hopeless, helpless
specimen, same species, but not of their kind.

His solid steel bucket sits two feet away, most
likely lined with a suggestive five or a ten, speaking
without voice to those who might come close, wallets
open, yet not close enough to meet its owner's eyes.

Shall I engage with this person in need, now only
two feet away? In my wallet I find a twenty, a five,
some ones. Now I am ready to make my move,
to do the right thing, close the gap between us,

both human, one hopelessly poor, the other a king. I
open my wallet, pull out the five, lean over, drop it in.
For a split second, our eyes connect.

STORMY WEATHER

Dawn Freight

Awakened from a sleep-shrouded state
by the distant growl of clickety-clacks, I
envision capsized grocery carts

along the bank of the ditch by the tracks
out of town, the forlorn tents of the homeless
hidden below with nowhere else to go, who

must endure the deafening blasts from the horn
of the freight. I stagger across the floor, splash
water on my face, move into the kitchen, turn on

the kettle, smell the pungent aromas
of tea from Ceylon. I open the front door,
retrieve today's news from our driveway:

"President defends tear-gassing children,
ripping babies from mothers' arms,
warns of chaos, injuries, even deaths."

Shredded Wheat

I stumble bleary to the kitchen for my morning meal.
A spoon of black tea, kettle switched to a boil, quick
trip to the driveway, I pick up the news from the street,
reach into the cupboard, pull out the shredded wheat.

The cereal is the same as it was seventy-five years before,
when I was an East Coast child of the Second World War.
It is the best no-sugar-added cereal in the store. I pour on
skimmed milk, add a strawberry or two, pick up the paper,
see what is new.

The headlines scream Santa Rosa fires, page-one stories of
devastation. Only eighty-four miles away, the survivors
look like me. Down in the corner a paragraph or two jumps
to the back page where there is even worse news.

Sixty North Korean nukes aimed over our nation, the
West Coast will be the first to go. Our harebrained self-
proclaimed genius has tweeted his reckless reply: "Bring
it on, we've got many more, you'll get total destruction."

I look down at my bowl, reach across the table, pick up
the brown sugar, scatter it over my shredded wheat.

Colors of a Winter Morning

We gather by the pond at misty December dawn for sightings
of migrating birds. Armed with telescopes and powerful
binocs, we spy on innocent wild creatures of flight.

Yellow-billed magpies (white breasts, dark blue tails)
strut boldly across our path, cedar waxwings
(black masks, pointed crowns, yellow-tipped tails)

perch vigilant atop a leaf-bare tree, a double-crested
cormorant (black, orange beaked) rests mid-pond
on a rock, flaps its wings, rises ominously into the sky.

Late morning, farmers proffer their wares at our outdoor
market downtown. Men, women, children, all ages, stroll
stall to stall, seek fresh-picked green, red, yellow

vegetables, fruit, salmon and sole. Shoppers are mostly
Caucasian or Asian, but olive-brown skins and the stall
for baba ghanoush and falafel can no longer be found.

Last night, a vandal smashed glass windows and doors
at the Islamic Center of our town, wrapped bacon
around the doorknobs.

The Daily Mail

Each weekday at ten and Saturdays too, I retrieve
our mail from one of the twelve cubby-hole boxes
that sit at the end of our street.

I pass by flowers with strange names (hydrangea and
alstroemeria), see pink roses opening their petals
under the drooping branches of our broad mayten tree.

I see I've neglected to fill the bird feeder and that the
red-berried green hedge that hides the fence between
our neighbor's property and our own needs trimming.

Suddenly I hear the grinding noise of a leaf blower
wielded by two Black men whose job is to keep our
street both clean and neat.

After I wave at the workmen and glance at the hedge,
I stroll up the street to our box, turn my key in the lock,
reach inside for our mail.

On top of the pile is a letter, return address Trump.
I place it at the bottom, carry it home, feed it
unopened into the shredder.

A Martian Enters the Apple Store

Since there is no door into the Apple Store,
I can walk right in and look around.
I look like them, so I blend right in,
check how they uphold our Galactic Plan.

The store is huge with twenty tables. Sleek
counters stretch along the walls. Above each
counter, parallel shelves hold thin rectangular
boxes, each used to issue news and commands.

When a box is held up to the eyes or an ear,
each earthling stooge receives hourly demands,
beamed earthwide from Our Dear Leader.

Strangely named "tweets" define his state
of mind at any time, day or night, his goal
to keep all earthlings under firm control.

T-shirted in green, friendly agents mix among
the earthling throng. Each one's emblem declares
authority at this Command Post Apple Store.

The agents seek out every citizen who's
here on a vital mission, to assure each one
is up to date on Our Dear Leader's urgent

news and tweeted commands. Throngs
of citizens stroll the halls, rectangular
boxes glued to their ears.

I walk back to the parking lot, take out my
transmitter, beam Galactic Command:
"All's well."

Alternative Facts

Comes now the winter of our discontent.
The Minotaur, let loose upon the land,
lets all know he brooks no dissent.
Reporters who cross him find themselves banned.
He could not care less for the sick, the homeless, the poor.
His huge-crowd claims are alternative facts
made up to support his delusions of grandeur—
numbers believed by none but his flacks.
His opponent's real margin of popularity,
falsely proclaimed as only fake news,
fades safely for him into deep obscurity.
Real numbers make him feel absurdly abused.
One hope remains: this phony occupant
becomes undone by the clause of emolument.

The Impostor

I.
We're into our fourth year of unending lies
from the impostor who in Lincoln's bed lies.

He tweets his falsehoods from six AM on.
"The largest-ever inaugural crowd," his first defining lie.

"Obama's lackeys sowed bugs in Trump Tower."
"Americans pay highest taxes ever," both ridiculous lies.

"The investigation of Russian collusion is all fabrication."
"The 'Fake News' media just wants to smear me," atrocious lies.

"Leakers are cowards and traitors; we'll find out who they are."
"The White House runs smooth despite the witch hunt," outrageous lies.

II.
He orders our border militia to protect at all cost our nation, America,
by ripping babies from the arms of migrating mothers from Central America.

He holds hostage their infants and children in wire-fenced compounds,
to assure they will never be citizens of our nation, America.

He defiles Liberty's enduring mission to hold high our national beacon,
embrace the huddled masses who yearn to be free in America.

When will the wheels of justice turn to banish this monster from our nation,
stop his reign of terror on the tempest-tossed many seeking refuge in America?

With growing concern, I observe this imposter through newspapers, TV,
long for the return of humanity, compassion in my birth nation, America.

BECOMING AND BEING A PHYSICIAN

Compassion

Formed and found in the human soul
lies the wellspring of compassion.
Seeing yourself in the other, the other
in yourself is the essence of compassion.

Selfless caring without condition for
voiceless unfortunate ones, feeling
the pain of another, accepting without
judging is compassion.

Caring for someone in need or in trouble,
putting yourself in another's shoes,
accepting and forgiving without condition
describes compassion.

When I became a doctor, my physician father
taught me what Dr. Francis Peabody had once
taught him: "The secret of the care of the patient
is in caring for the patient" with compassion.

First Patient

At the end of my second medical school year, a fifty-year-old woman with multiple sclerosis volunteered as a subject for my course in physical diagnosis. As I walked to her house, new doctor's bag in hand, I recalled the times when my physician father had invited me, age six, to ride with him on house calls in the New England town of my childhood.

I rang my patient's bell, heard her shuffling footsteps approaching the door. Her smile and tremulous extended right hand told me she was pleased to play a vital role in my medical education.

As we sat across from each other in her living room, I saw that her vision was skewed, only her left eye meeting mine. She told me her symptoms had begun in her mid-thirties, first with clumsiness of her right hand and episodic clouding of vision in the right eye. Later, she developed variable weakness and stiffness in her left leg, occasional dizziness, and tired quickly while doing housework.

Examining her starting with her head, I found that her right eye lagged the left as I passed my index finger left to right, up and down. She had comparative weakness of her left arm when pulled against mine, strong knee and ankle tendon reflex responses in her right leg, and an involuntary jerking response to my pressure on the sole of her left foot.

When I had completed my exam, thanked her, and departed, I felt extremely indebted for her unstinting gift to my medical education. The complexities of becoming and being a physician had just begun to sink in.

Liftoff

On February 20, 1962, I began my clinical rotation in obstetrics as a fourth-year medical student in Rochester, New York. In the doctors' room awaiting my first patient, I watched the liftoff of the Friendship 7 spacecraft on a black-and-white television as John Glenn became the first American astronaut to circle the earth.

I was called to the delivery room as Glenn was ending the first of three orbits. The attending faculty obstetrician stood by while I observed the infant's head emerging through our patient's expanding and perfectly circular birth canal. My faculty supervisor guided me through my first hands-on delivery, a baby girl, whom I gently lifted and passed off to the nurse at my side.

Fifty years later, a medical faculty member in Sacramento, I was asked to speak with a hospital administrator about a program I had initiated to support the nutritional needs of hospitalized patients. She told me she had learned from my curriculum vitae that I had attended medical school in the city where she had been born. As a child, she had been told she had arrived soon after John Glenn's first of three orbits of the earth.

First Stint in the ER

A month into my internship, a fortyish man arrived in the ER,
clutching his belly after ten days of worsening pain. His
abdomen was tender throughout, his bowel sounds few.

His anxious wife said she was sure an old ulcer had flared.
Though she had plied him with Maalox, a tablespoon five times
each day, his pain just got worse, more frequent, intense.

A respected church elder, he had often flirted with the ladies.
His furious wife was certain he was up to no good, or even
worse, when he left home after dark and returned hours later.

Although he had normal blood tests, an abdominal X-ray
outlined his large bowel in white, as if he had received a
barium enema. Yet, there was no record of this procedure.

My year-older resident thought he knew the answer. A different
liquid could appear on the X-ray as white. Confronted, the wife
admitted she had added arsenic to each Maalox dose, so the

more pain he got, the more arsenic he took. This story ended
poorly when his kidneys stopped working. Dialysis was not
yet perfected. The patient died. His wife was arrested, indicted.

The Last Iron Lungs

In 1963, the springtime of my intern year, I
rotated onto the polio ward. The new Sabin
oral vaccine arrived too late for the worst-off
patients, who were doomed to spend the rest
of their lives in iron lungs.

In these body-sized devices lay the patients
whose chests could not expand, who could
not inhale enough oxygen to stay alive. The
diagnosis of poliomyelitis continued as a
sentence of death.

I watched over the few survivors by listening to their
lungs at least once an hour. To do this, I reached my
stethoscope-holding hand through an opening in the
side of each iron lung, so I could distinguish clear
breathing from gurgles of failing respiration.

The night nurse was an avid Cleveland Indians fan,
whose favorite player, Mudcat Grant, had transferred
to the Majors from the Negro League. Mudcat had
played in the All-Star Game and became the
first Black pitcher to win twenty games in a season.

I liked to imagine that my iron-lung patients
were also avid Cleveland fans who listened
to radio broadcasts of every home game,
silently cheering for Mudcat along with
the recorded cheers of the Indians' fans.

Quid Pro Quo

My patient was a sixty-five-year-old city councilman whose
epigastric pain had persisted for three months. Obese,
his dietary habits were unrestrained.

In the early 1970s, few antacids had been invented.
Liquid Maalox was ineffectual, probably because
he could out-eat its antacid effect.

Influential in city government, he complained that he had waited
ten minutes in traffic to turn into our city hospital's parking lot.
By the next week, a new streetlight was installed at that very spot.

To obtain precise medical information, I arranged to measure his
gastric acidity, then considered an essential step in diagnosing
a suspected gastric ulcer.

As I began to insert a small-caliber tube though his nose,
my patient broke out in a sweat and said, "Doc, I'm not
feeling so good," and started to sway on the gurney.

I stopped what I was doing, held him tightly around his shoulders,
eased him onto his back, called for intravenous fluids, and
monitored his falling blood pressure and racing pulse.

He came to after ten minutes of intravenous saline infusion and said,
"Doc, that was one heck of a test. Is there some way I can repay you?"
After a thoughtful silence, I told him about the cracks in the city
sidewalk in front of my house. A week later, they were fixed.

Final Board Exam

When I opened the door to her hospital room, my
patient was on the telephone with her son, talking
about her daughter-in-law and the well-being
of her grandchildren.

This was the last of my National Board Exams,
a three-part grilling: the first two multiple choice,
the final a physical exam of a willing patient. If I
failed any one of them, I would not get a medical
license. I would not become a practicing physician.

I had completed medical school, internship, residency,
and half of my specialty training. My volunteer patient,
an elderly woman, lay in her bed, discharge pending,
oblivious to my need to perform a physical examination.

After thirty minutes, she returned the phone to its cradle, and
I quickly unpacked my stethoscope to examine her heart, her
breathing, and abdominal sounds; my ophthalmoscope to check
her eyes; my flashlight to examine her mouth and tongue. I felt
the edge of her liver, tapped the reflexes of her elbows and knees.

Twenty minutes later, the soft stethoscope sounds
of her abdomen were shattered by the ringing telephone, and
she returned to family issues. A knock on the door told me
my time was up. Three middle-aged MDs strolled in,
asked me to show them how I had examined her liver.

Three weeks of anxiety went by. At last the awaited
letter appeared: "Dear Dr—, we are pleased to inform. . . ."
was all I needed to read. I had passed.

The Korean Soldier

A fifty-five-year-old Korean man arrived at the ER after vomiting blood in the night. Called the next morning to consult in our intensive care unit, I reviewed his chart and pulled back the curtain surrounding his bed. He was barely responsive with rapid heartbeats, one hundred per minute, and a slight fever. His blood pressure was normal, his mouth breathing regular with normal rate. Carefully rolling back his eyelids, I observed yellow eyeballs and found normally reactive pupils.

When I pulled the bedsheet down to his waist, I found spider-like clusters of veins across his chest and upper abdomen. The liver was firm and enlarged while gentle tapping on each side of his belly produced a rolling fluid wave. The tip of his spleen could be felt in the left upper abdomen. His lower legs were thin sticks, his ankles mildly swollen.

Laboratory tests from his midnight visit to the ER were consistent with liver failure: marked elevation of the serum bilirubin and alkaline phosphatase, low serum albumin, and moderately elevated blood ammonia.

My patient suffered from long-term disease of the liver, its cause uncertain. His wife arrived and filled in historical gaps: He never drank alcohol because it caused the severe facial flushing common to Asians. Thirty-five years before, he had fought for the South in the Korean War. As the North Korean and Chinese troops pushed the South Korean and American soldiers below the thirty-eighth parallel, he had received a deep bullet wound in his thigh.

A US Army field hospital in South Korea had treated him with five units of blood during surgical removal of the bullet and repair of the wound. Most likely the long-ago blood transfusions had carried the virus that had led to his liver failure. New laboratory results were positive for serum hepatitis B.

After the war, my patient married the Korean nurse who had cared for him in the field hospital. They had one child, a daughter, now twenty years old. They had emigrated to San Francisco four years before to be close to relatives and in time for their brilliant daughter to attend nearby Stanford University. During the postwar years, he wrote a memoir of his wartime recollections which his wife and daughter had translated into English. Later, they transformed his life story into an epic poem in heroic verse.

I continued to see my patient on my daily rounds. He became more responsive, but his confusion never completely cleared, and his laboratory tests remained abnormal. On day seven, his breathing gradually slowed and stopped, his wife and daughter at his bedside.

When I talked with them about his diseased liver that could never recover, his wife presented me his lifetime memoir in English verse. Later that year, I learned that their daughter had enrolled in the first-year class of the medical school where I was a faculty physician.

Sidewalk Shuffle

Six months before, he had led a group
of interested folk, including me, on an
exploration of fauna and foliage on
the other side of the well-known creek
that winds its way through our valley.

He had led us up a steep trail with switchbacks
progressing ever higher. The creek receding
with every turn, a panorama of hills and
lakes ahead was a well-earned reward.

Now, at our twice-monthly coffee shop
meeting, I was met with a blank stare when
I looked up to begin our discussion.

As we picked up our menus, his pill-rolling
fingers and thumbs spelled Parkinson's disease,
confirmed as we departed when I saw that
his walk had become a continuous shuffle.

Years later, his disease now worsening, his
sidewalk gait had progressed to stumbling.
When I called out his name,
he did not respond.

Our Boarder with Celiac Disease

I listened with care to her history of weight loss, grain aversion, abdominal cramps, frequent toilet trips. Her grandfather had complained of the same symptoms for years before he died. Her body weight for her height was fifteen percent below normal. She had no rashes, her skin texture was normal, her tongue was smooth, and her neck unremarkable.

Her lungs were clear and heart normal, but the abdominal sounds were gurgling rushes. There was minimal pinprick sensation in her lower legs. Her lab tests showed mild macrocytic cell anemia with low serum folate and normal vitamin B12 levels. I suspected celiac disease and proposed a complete evaluation, a complicated task since she lived a four-hour drive away.

I would need a three-day fecal collection to quantify intestinal malabsorption, a five-hour urine collection to measure d-xylose absorption, and a biopsy of the surface of the small intestine. My wife agreed to have my patient live in our guest room near a private bathroom for three-day fecal and five-hour urine collections.

Four days later, my patient rode with me to the hospital lab to deposit the samples and to complete a blood draw for genetic testing. That afternoon, I performed a tube-capsule biopsy of the surface of the small intestine. All tests confirmed celiac disease. A gluten-free diet was instituted, and she responded well to this treatment at home.

Each time I pass her town as I travel north, I recall my patient's stay with my family. I think of her pioneer ancestors who may have been afflicted with her disease for generations before it had been discovered.

EKPHRASIS

Between Heaven and Hell

If you go to Madrid, you should visit the Museo del Prado.
Once inside, if you proceed to a room near the middle, you
can view the masterpiece triptych of mankind as we behaved
five hundred years ago, conceivably the same way as today.

On the leftmost panel, you will find God's introduction of
Adam to Eve, just sprung from Adam's rib, while several
cats chewing on mice foretell the perils ahead. In the large
center panel, dozens of nubile naked women preen in various
poses, hoping for penetration by one or more uninterested men,

some of whom choose fellatio or flagellation instead. Other men
parade their prowess while riding a variety of animals around
a shallow pool containing naked women. The panel on the right
depicts the horrors of hell awaiting the errant men, spears thrust
through their chests, preamble to being thrown into fires eternal.

Five hundred years later, man's seeking for sex and power remains
unchanged. Our narcissistic president is entrenched as never before,
the nukes he controls stand ready for war, a phone call away. Yet, the
calla lilies that beckon in bloom below my window remind me that
sexual desire springs eternal.

The Garden of Earthly Delights
Hieronymus Bosch, 1504

The Boozy Soldier

Ruddy cheeked, boozy with tattered vest
and barely balanced glass of genever,
he extends a shaky hand to say:

"Since you have bought my last drink,
I will tell you of places I have been,
the Amsterdam whores I have known,

the Spaniards I have killed
as a soldier of Orange, with
blunderbuss and sword."

He has staggered into the tavern from
wintry cold, from seeking alms
along snow-fringed canals,

scraps of food tossed out for dogs.
Wall-eyed and thin, he lives only
for his next drink,

hoping to sleep it off inside,
not on the cobblestone streets,
puking up blood in the gutter,

possessed by demons and ghosts
of comrades long gone.

The Merry Drinker
Franz Hals, 1628-30

Three Sheets to the Wind

Holding high his half-empty wineglass, Papa is roaring drunk,
oblivious to the messy dining table, the half-eaten roast, the
howling refrain from the family dog.

Mama, her cleavage exposed, sings from the sheet of music in
drunken grandma's hands, while the babe sips along with the rest,
bangs a spoon on the table to the merry tunes of the piper and flute.

In the foreground, the oldest daughter pours wine for her ten-
year-old sister, who stands ready to swig it all down. A half-
empty jug awaits them both on the tiled floor nearby.

Two uncles sit in a corner, each one having had his fill. They
smoke their pipes while eying their niece, each one hoping
he will become the first one to arrive at her side.

Above them, a sheet of paper pinned to the wall is inscribed with
a Dutch proverb: "The Young Will Inherit the Sins of their Elders."
Bacchus, leaning across the windowsill, has seen it all before.

The Merry Family
Jan Steen, 1668

Strange Copulation

Anticipation turns to mounting desire.
She draws its downy neck closer and sighs.
Grasping wings assure it will sire,
when, in wordless dance, she parts her thighs.
While she fulfills her secret assignation,
the cuckold king impatiently awaits,
oblivious, preparing her impregnation
in their rock-bound castle far off in the haze.
The bastard babes look up in complicity.
What meets their gaze will become inheritance.
Their destinies are promiscuity,
endless warring humanity's dance.
From Helen of Troy to weapons of depopulation,
all these become fruit of this strange copulation.

Leda and the Swan
Cesare da Sesto after Leonardo, 1515–1520

Red Stockings

She is exhausted from her nighttime job,
sitting alone at her red light-rimmed window,
beckoning lonely men with inviting eyes,
hooking in the carousing johns who roam

the famous Amsterdam street half drunk
and the furtive innocents taking care they
will not be seen glancing up at her
window, each one ready for plucking.

She will soon count her earnings, putting aside
all she can hide from her greedy expectant
pimp. Slippers tossed on the floor, she pulls off
her red stockings, garter marks left behind.

Still wearing her warm cloak for protection
against the freezing Amsterdam winter,
chamber pot half full, devoted little dog on
her pillow, she is ready to crawl into bed.

Woman at her Toilet
Jan Steen, 1655-60

FAMILY AND FRIENDS

Then and Now

During World War II, my Pa, a US Army medical officer,
took care of sick soldiers in Italy, while my older brother,
age eleven, and I, age eight, played at being soldiers in the
nearby New England woods. Late afternoons, I listened

to our scratchy Victrola-radio (no TV yet) in the living
room for the latest wartime news, which came on just
before my favorite programs: *Batman and Robin, Tom
Mix*, and *The Lone Ranger*. Each one advertised a breakfast

cereal that I insisted my mother should buy. I kept a growing
supply of comic books, each costing a nickel at the newspaper
store downtown. Batman and Superman kept us safe while
the Nazis and Japanese were diabolical fiends, destroying

all in their way. So it was, in 1945, that I witnessed epic
events through radio reports, including our President's
death in April, the conquest of Germany in May, and the
Japanese surrender in August at Tokyo Bay.

Seventy-five years have passed, my children and
grandchildren live far away, my first career is over, my
second and last on its way, and more and more friends are
gone. Will, a fighter pilot in the War, died last week at

age ninety-four, and Lee, a former midshipman at Tokyo
Bay, expired at ninety-three. Milt, who served in a mountain
brigade in Italy, is still going strong at one hundred and two
but can no longer stand without help.

My mother died in her bed in 2006 at age ninety-nine,
while my father passed from leukemia, age seventy-eight
in 1984. Next year I will outlive my older brother, who died
three years ago of kidney cancer at age eighty-three.

Whispers of God

To the memory of Raymond Coppock, 1922-2016

The Nazi forces of evil slowly crossed the field. Their
machine guns stuttered, their tanks no more concealed.
The blast would ensure that none would survive.
Amazed, he found himself both well and alive.

The man who'd stood by him was dead in their hole.
Though frozen with fear, he stayed fixed on his goal:
to prevail with courage throughout the war. Their
fields were shredded, their villages no more

than giant heaps of stones and broken glass.
All the people had fled, their futures had passed.
He found himself standing near an ancient spire,
a cathedral rising from smoldering fires.

He entered alone and stood still in the nave.
The holy emptiness whispered his name,
which echoed throughout this fortress of God.
He lived from then on in constant awe.

Bend in the River

My friend the squirrel sits on a branch, peers
though my window in late afternoon to be certain
that I am still alive. I'm ready to begin my journey
down the river as it rounds its final bend.

Upstream, it flows past our first house where
I carried each of you in my womb more than
sixty-five years ago. Later, I made sure that none

of us would starve from lack of eggs or milk
from the chickens and goats we kept when
your Pa was away in the War.

You are all here to take turns at the word games I love,
though now I lose more than I win. I've long
forgiven your hurts as you have mine. You've all
come here to hold me close as my end draws near.

When I close my eyes, I will float down the river. Once
past its bend, I will enter the harbor and sea, become one
with eternal waves crashing against the rocky shore.

Why Did You Have to Die?

Q
Three years older, you were always big brother.
We shared the boys' room while we were still growing.
Each night in our beds when you turned out the lights,
you told tales of the monster that dwelled in the black
attic closet just over our heads at the top of the stairs,
ready to pounce and devour if ever I opened its door.
I had never thought you would be gone so long
before your time, before mine.

A
I never thought I would die so soon, though I'd led my life
to the full before the attic monster broke loose, as we knew
sooner or later it would. In many a different guise, it has
wreaked its havoc, taken many lives, including my own.
We should be glad we had each other as brothers
until my fate arrived. You must be grateful
for every day as long as you remain alive.

Letter to My Dying Brother

When I was six, I watched you, age nine,
almost blow off your hand while lighting
a Fourth-of-July cherry bomb and determined
I would always be the good son.

Each night before we turned out the light
in the boys' room we shared, you told me
the last dirty joke you had learned. We played
at being soldiers in World War II, while
our Pa was away for four long years.

When I was sixteen, you watched over me
on a cross-country drive with two other guys.
In a basement joint on Bourbon Street, you
showed me how to sip my first beer while
watching a stripper tease off her clothes.

When our parents divorced in our teenage years,
we went different ways, yours career army,
mine to learn and practice our Pa's profession.
Each with new family, we lived on opposite coasts.

Fourteen years ago, I was first to get the male cancer.
Two years later you got it too. I told you the way
you should follow, but true to form, you chose
a different path to be rid of the cherry bomb within.

When you wrote that new cancerous growths
glowed like Christmas tree lights on your MRI,
I knew that soon there would be no more
emails signed Bro1 and Bro2.

Paean to My Younger Sister

Each of us maneuvered our childhoods with
silver spoons in our mouths, grew up in a
sheltered suburb of Boston, attended
the best private schools.

Big brother and I were merciless teasers. We
made you cry by hiding your precious toys
or by holding your favorite stuffed animal
out the window of the moving family car.

Our family came apart when our Pa took
a job in LA, moved us cross country, and
divorced our Mum, who took you back East
to our New England roots.

Six years later, both of us attending the same
college, you fixed me up with the French
professor's daughter, a teenage girl well
known by other boys to "go all the way."

As adults, our siblinghood grew stronger. With
a PhD, you taught English to multiracial New
York City students, edited a book on aging

called *Views from the Bridge*, painted landscapes and
seascapes that rival those of our artist grandfather.
Your paintings of horses are widely acclaimed.

Three weeks ago, I learned you were in the
hospital with a rare disease of the heart. Though
we now live on opposite coasts, you are foremost
in my thoughts, my always inspiring younger sister.

Eulogy for Al

Dedicated to the memory of Albert Woods Moore, 1921-1997

My brother-in-law, investment banker,
tennis tournament winner, seventy-six,
retired, laid low by Parkinson's disease
that led to a fractured hip, was finally
felled by a heart attack.

His funeral took place in Belfast, Maine,
amid ice-covered roadways, broken
branches, downed power lines—still recalled
as the great ice storm—in January
of the third-to-last year of the nineties.

Freezing, we gathered in a church, each
to tell how we had known this man. While he
had called me "doctor," I had called him
"counselor," an advisor to my son on financial
careers, sharing my pride in his future success.

On a long-ago ride with Al at my side, I took
my 280Z to ninety on country roads. To reward
my guts, he sent me a windbreaker emblazoned
with his company logo. Years later, though he
whipped me at tennis, I took four games, the
first sign of the assault of his disease.

For ten years he cursed the shuffle, the mumble,
the multiple drugs that tore up his mind. Though
we spoke of salmon fishing in Maine, each of us
knew this would never happen. Missing his brake-
pedal one snowy night, he crashed his car into a tree.

On a phone call the day before he died,
he spoke of reunion in an incoherent way,
half conversing with spirits I knew he had joined
in the crystal landscape that surrounded us all
in that frozen winter church in Belfast, Maine.

Sierra Butte

Dedicated to the memory of Eldridge Morton Moores III, 1938-2018

He reveled in our pristine surroundings ingrained in his very
being, on a summer weekend with wives at a North Yuba cabin
midway to the ridge of his beloved Sierra Nevada, where I showed
him how to catch a fish while standing on a mid-river rock.

As a frantic trout fought to survive my fake fly hooked
in its mouth, I handed him my flyrod, taught him to keep
tension hard on the line, to control the jerking fish, to
prevent its potential downstream run, to hold tight till

it tired, to pull it up to our sides. I slid it into my hand-held
net, brought it up to shore, hit its head hard with a rock,
then sliced out its guts. Together, we presented our fish
to our wives for our first evening meal of the trip.

Next morning, we set out, a mountain to climb, his forte,
five miles by car to a parking lot, a half-mile hike up
a dirt road to its end, then the final ascent to a fire lookout
at eight thousand six hundred feet, the top of Sierra Butte.

Hiking up the trail was a breeze for him and his wife, found
resting in shade near the final ascent. Assuming they had
completed the climb, I advanced to the base of a firm metal
ladder, the approach to the lookout station, a panorama ahead.

Looking up, I saw two chasms to cross, each bridged by a
ladder with rungs a foot and one half apart, two hundred to get
to the top. After three hesitant steps, a vast chasm unfolded,
hundreds of rocky feet down. Heart racing, sweat pouring,

I retreated to firm ground to rejoin the others for the walk
back down. Years later, the topic of mountain climbs emerged
at one of our old guys' meetings, specifically the views from
the top. When I related my failed ascent to the group, he
looked up and simply responded: "I chickened out, too."
This was but one of the times that we bonded.

Visiting Will

Dedicated to the memory of Willard Stanley Lotter, 1924-2019

A US Navy vet of World War II, he played fullback on the UC Berkeley football team, Rose Bowl '49, and coached varsity soccer, baseball, and football at UC Davis at intervals from '52 to '93. He married Jane, his college sweetheart, for a sixty-nine-year marriage. He was the father of four sons, the grandfather of two girls and a boy.

From '65 through '67, Will and Jane volunteered for the Peace Corps in Malawi, where he directed its programs, then trained volunteers in Nepal while on the way home. Fifteen years later, he made multiple trips in support of human rights in Guatemala, Nicaragua, and El Salvador.

At great personal risk during the era of genocides of Guatemalan villages, he escorted two witnesses and their families to safety. In 2000, he and Jane cofounded our city's Religious Community for Sanctuary, for which they received its Peace and Justice Award.

As a consulting doctor, I cared briefly for both Will and Jane as they grew into old age. I teased Will about the time my UC Berkeley son scored the winning goal against his UC Davis soccer team. Two years ago, Jane died, and from then on Will lived in severe depression, cared for by his eldest son and African daughter-in-law.

From time to time, I dropped in to offer friendship and support. Such a day was Christmas Eve, when Will's son met me in the living room of their house. Neither tree nor bunting matched the season. Led to his bed, I encountered Will's sheet-shrouded body, uncertain if he was dead or asleep. When I announced my presence, he uncovered his unshaven face and broke into a wide smile of recognition. From under his covers. he reached out an ancient hand, held mine tight.

My Lasting Life Partner

Excelling in all that arrived on her plate, she
was a PR exec with a vast intellect. We came
together at a museum exhibit (it may have been
Renoir). She could translate my scientific research
into plain English a nonscientist could follow.

I arranged for a snip vasectomy; she tossed her
diaphragm out the window of a New York skyscraper
hotel. Over the phone, she taught me to cook
spaghetti with sautéed garlic. She brought me along on
business trips: Saltsjöbaden, London, Canterbury.

Within six months, she became my heart's
desire, and I committed to all she inspired.
She cut her ties to her New York career,
moved in with me on the opposite coast.

I read my first poem, one of renewal,
as part of our marriage vows.
Our lives remain entwined.

On-Time Arrival

Before it's too late, and I might
take a wrong step, trip, take a fall,
arrive so late that we miss our flight,

I make my way to the assuring sight
of our car and give my wife a call
before it's too late, so she might

maneuver through traffic jams and lights,
careful to stay in the lane, not hit a wall,
nor arrive so late that we miss our flight,

drive the interstate in early sunlight,
skipping breakfast to bring us all
the way before it's too late and we might,

despite the traffic, avoid the plight
of being no-shows, as if we had the gall
to arrive so late that we miss our flight.

I know you can do it, my precious wife,
avoid the embarrassing drop of the ball,
arrive on time at the gate so we might
not be so late that we miss our flight.

THE LAST CHAPTER

When You Consider Your Aging Brain

Inspired by Shakespeare's "Sonnet 15"

When you think about all living things
that capture awareness if but for a second,
each stage of aging maintains its own ring,
but only as long as your future years beckon.
Though memory dwindles each day of each year,
your present plans for each future event
retain their places though often less clear.
Enjoy each day, your aging will not relent.
Do not pretend your foggy mind will sustain
all its circuits, no longer instantaneous.
What clarity remains in your shrinking brain
must be focused: Avoid the extraneous.
Yet, however your advancing age is spent,
you cannot predict the when of your final descent.

Some Things About Eighty

Your wife drives the car, often as not.
　　You pump the gas, check all the tires.
　　　　You donate your ten-speed bike
　　　　　　to your church auction.

Eighty is sometimes forgetting
　　names of relatives, neighbors, and friends,
　　　　some of the places you've been,
　　　　　　the insides of houses you've lived in.

Eighty is failing to recall
　　where you are when you wake while traveling,
　　　　details of what you must do today, while making
　　　　　　sure not to wear yesterday's clothes,
　　　　　　　　or where you left your keys.

Eighty is deciding
　　where to place your feet when walking,
　　　　to keep your eyes on each sidewalk crack
　　　　　　where you might stumble and land on your face,
　　　　　　　　how to hold tight on the handrail while climbing stairs.

Eighty is forgetting to
　　put your hearing aids in every morning,
　　　　take your pills three times a day,
　　　　　　clip your overgrown toenails.

Eighty is remembering that
　　your grandfathers lived into their late nineties,
　　　　your mother lived till ninety-nine
　　　　　　but your father died at seventy-eight,
　　　　　　　　your older brother last year at eighty-three.

Boxed In

You start to feel the walls closing in when
you take a tumble the second time, let us say
on a sidewalk when you trip on a crack, or
worse when you forget to step up on a curb.

You start to feel the walls closing in
when your mind begins to wander at the
crucial time as your car does the same
instead of staying inside your lane.

Perhaps there is a real solution: let
your wife take the wheel, give up
your freedom, accede to her pleas to move
into your town's retirement home, as
dismal and dreary as it may seem.

When you have settled in and your life is
no longer your own, restricted to long
dark corridors of impending doom, you will
know you have come full circle when,
once again, you begin to drool.

Paean to Mum

When I was four years old and three feet
tall, you threw yourself between me and an
attacking Adirondack deer, hell-bent on
protecting her nearby fawn.

When I was six at the start of the War, with
our Pa overseas to care for sick soldiers, you
held us safe from Nazi subs, kept a victory
garden, chickens, and goats.

When I started first grade, you taught me
to do right after I copied a wrong answer
from the little girl who sat in front.

When I was twelve, you marched into
my prep school class to tell my teacher
his homework was just too hard, then
praised me later for doing it well.

When I was thirteen and we moved to LA,
Pa's divorce decree and your losing me
caused you many sad years, till you
had started your own new career.

When I was sixteen, you stifled your tears
when my older brother, two of his friends,
and I set off to drive Boston-LA in three days.

When I finished college at twenty-one and
hitchhiked through western Europe alone,
you freed me to lead a vagabond life by
keeping your fears to yourself.

When I married my first wife at age twenty-two,
you questioned whether I knew what I had done, yet
accepted my choice.

When you invited my second wife-to-be to your
kitchen for tea, regaled her with stories of me as
a boy, displayed my grandfather's portrait of me
as a child, you showed her how much I was loved.

When you took to your bed at age 98, I made cross-
country trips whenever your hospice nurse called and
spent hours reading to you from my favorite childhood
books that you'd kept in your closet for more than fifty years.

When one winter day you asked my brother if you had made
it to one hundred, he replied, "Six months to go." You simply
said, "Good enough," and drifted away.

About Charles Halsted

The grandson of a professional artist and son of a physician, Charles Halsted grew up in Dedham, Massachusetts, a Boston suburb, and Los Angeles. He attended Stanford University (BA, 1958) and the University of Rochester School of Medicine & Dentistry (MD, 1962), followed by internship and residency training at Cleveland Metropolitan General Hospital (1962-66). To fulfill his military obligation, he served as a research scientist at the US Naval Medical Research Unit in Cairo, Egypt (1966-68). Upon his return to the US, he pursued specialty training in gastroenterology at Johns Hopkins Hospital in Baltimore (1968-70).

His distinguished academic medical career at the Baltimore City Hospital (1970-73) and the UC Davis School of Medicine (1974-2016) included clinical practice, teaching, and continuously funded biomedical research. His medical publications included 105 original research papers, two books, and dozens of book chapters, review articles, and editorials. He was elected a Fellow of the American Association for the Advancement of Science, the American College of Physicians, the American Gastroenterological Association, the American Association for the Study of Liver Diseases, and the American Society for Nutrition Sciences and a Member of the American Society for Clinical Investigation. For ten years, he served as Editor-in-Chief of the *American Journal of Clinical Nutrition.*

To prepare for his new career in poetry, he enrolled in classes taught by local poets, then completed twelve online poetry courses offered by Stanford Continuing Studies. In addition, he participated in the Community of Writers at Squaw Valley Poetry Workshop and the Poetry Workshop with Edward Hirsch at Tor House in Carmel. Other writing conferences included the Fishtrap Gathering of Writers, three Taos Writers Conferences, and the Catamaran Writing Conference. His eighty-plus poems have appeared in more than thirty journals. His chapbook, *Breaking Eighty*, and two full-length poetry books, *Extenuating Circumstances* and the present volume, are published by Finishing Line Press.